A supplementary book to 'THE THEORY OF IDENTITIES: SOCIAL STRATIFICATION'

WRITTEN BY

ARYAN SANGEETH

PUBLISHED BY

SANGEETH D RAJAN

ARYANBOOKS INDIA

Contact us via Website: www.aryansangeeth.wordpress.com

<u>First Edition</u>: January 2022, Revised on September 2023

<u>Second Edition</u>: March 2025 (Removal of Index & advertisement, change in font and font size, error correction)

<u>NOTICE</u>

- *The cover page and price may vary according to the location where the book is sold.*
- *The author is not responsible for any damage to the book or any torn pages of the book.*
- *The book is fully written in India by the author.*
- *This book is currently available only in English language.*
- *The book is available in eBook, paperback and hardcover format.*
- *The book doesn't use any image from internet and all the shapes are created through computer.*
- *The author doesn't stand in favor or against any identity. He is neutral and deeply respects all identities of the people.*
- *This book is based on author's observations and assumptions.*
- *Identity spirited and sensitive people are requested not to see this book as a critic's vision. The author doesn't criticize any identity and the book is based only on reality.*
- *Although this book follows a non-academic approach, it is most preferred for the social scientists and researchers especially for those who work in the field of Humanities and Administration.*
- *The readers are suggested to read "THE THEORY OF IDENTITIES: SOCIAL STRATIFICATION" written by the same author for understanding this book properly.*
- *Efforts have been taken to write this book in simple words for the readers to grasp the meaning correctly.*
- *The content of the book is based more on Indian society.*
- *Feedback for this book can be given through this email: aryanbooksindia@gmail.com. We are happy to get review from the readers who can directly communicate with us through this email.*

Dedicated to

My father who has given me a lot of support in writing this book. Dad has also given me confidence and strength to explore the world and understand the life situations.

-ARYAN SANGEETH

FOREWORD

The previous book "THE THEORY OF IDENTITIES: SOCIAL STRATIFICATION" is about primary or 'first of all' identities such as religion, caste, class, race etc. This book explains the primary identities which are able to convert to secondary and vice versa. These identities also have discrimination within it. There are seven such identities. That is why this book is named as "THE RAINBOW OF DISCRIMINATORY IDENTITIES". We know that there are seven colours for a rainbow-Violet, Indigo, Blue, Green, Yellow, Orange and Red (VIBGYOR). The rainbow perhaps appear in the sky after rains. Similarly, there are identities which are so linked to each other that they together seem to appear in life. Some tend to discriminate the colours of rainbow by giving preference to a colour or by saying one favourite colour. This is inequality and the same case happens in identities also. If a natural rainbow is formed by scattering or due to sunlight and atmospheric conditions, the man-made identity rainbow is formed by social diversity and unacceptance to each other's identity.

The main aim of this book is to explain each of the identity in rainbow separately and to explain its structure, functioning and mechanism. The merits and demerits of upholding the present pattern of identity interaction will be also discussed.

Author

ARYAN SANGEETH

PREFACE

In this book, we discuss about the factors dealing with identity rainbow such as quality and quantity. The quality means the origin, experience and simplicity of identity while the quantity means the number of people having that identity. This identity rainbow is very important to understand the secondary identities. The secondary identities become primary in a wider stretch of rainbow. For example, the language is secondary to people if the people speaking the same language live together. But if there are different language speaking people in one area, it becomes a primary identity as people start praising their own language to defeat others.

USER MANUAL

It is advisable to read from the first chapter to know different aspects of discriminatory identities. The page numbers are given at the bottom of the page. The title of the book is at the top of every pages. This book is written in modern format which contains many help tools like those mentioned above. If you get any doubt regarding the theory, you can contact author or use internet facility if you have.

<u>ACKNOWLEDGEMENTS</u>

Special Thanks to my mother Anju Sangeeth for facilitating me for writing this book. Big Thanks to Arjun Sangeeth for illustrating and typewriting the book. A small thanks to Wikipedia for helping me to gain much more knowledge. Thanks also to NCERT Textbook as it provided a good source for me to understand in detail.

<u>CONTENTS</u>

CHAPTER-1

LINGUISTIC IDENTITY

The language of a person is regarded as an 'identity' as to what group of speakers he/she belong. Creation of this language identity is of two ways:-

i. An individual created language which gets followers that lead to the spread of the language throughout the society in different directions. This language with course of time becomes the mother tongue of a group. This way is very difficult in modern times.

ii. Struggle created language is the language that people together created as a group for making easiness in communication.

There is also convergence and divergence of language. Convergence means a language combines with another language to form a single language. Divergence means a language split to form many languages.

Eg:-(1)European languages were formed by divergence of Latin.

(2)Hindustani was formed by convergence of Hindi, Urdu and other Indian languages.

LEVELS OF LINGUISTIC IDENTITY

1.Language Family Identity

A group of languages having similar characteristics and common words are a part of single identity. This family through divergence may have led to large number of languages.

Eg:-Indo-European(Aryan),Dravidian, Austric.

2.Single Language Identity

A language very distinct from others and do not resemble each other is a single language.

Eg:-Hindi do not match with Tamil.

3.Dialect Identity

If divergence of language occur in its sub divisions, it will lead to formation of dialects. Dialects are just having a very few number of different words or a change in the way of speaking style.

Eg:-Hindi have 17 dialects like Bhojpuri, Brajbhasha, Awadhi, Bundeli, Rajasthani etc.

MIXING OF LINGUISTIC IDENTITY OR A MIX OF HOMOGENOUS LANGUAGE

Adding a different language with one language lead to improper language which is used for showing nobility.

Eg:- Hinglish (Hindi + English)

STAMMER IDENTITY

People usually consider stammer as a disorder. But indeed it is an identity of people as there are a lot of people who stammers. This identity has to be given respect and the ill treatment to stammer identity shall be given punishments by the law. The only problem with this identity is that people who stammer are unevenly distributed throughout the globe.

MANAGEMENT OF LINGUISTIC IDENTITIES

Five Models can be used for the management of Linguistic identities.

1. National Language Model

This model makes a particular language as first or primary language for everyone legally.

Advantages:

i. Unity and Integrity of the nation.
ii. Communication becomes easier.
iii. 'Similarity' overriding the equality- All speak same language instead of giving equal status to many language which would have made multiple identities.

Limitations:

i. Loss of diversity and superiority of one language.
ii. Disregard and alienation of those who are reluctant to change their language.
iii. Extinction of other languages and its culture.

2. Linguistic States Model

Dividing the country into provinces or territories or regions based on language.

Advantage:

i. Federating units will declare their own state language and this will preserve their originality.
ii. Comfortability for people to speak up their thoughts and ideas.
iii. Conservation of the script and talk of a language.

Limitations:

i. Threat to security of nation if regionalism exceeds.
ii. Autonomy demands will increase.

3. Secession and Disintegration Model

Dividing a country into different separate countries.

Advantages:

i. Achievement of one nation, one language
ii. End of civil war or internal disturbances.

Limitations:

i. Minority language speaker remains as people refuse to leave their homes.
ii. Country becoming smaller and creating non-viable economies.

4. Linguistic District/Village Model

Reserving a town or countryside for one language speakers.

Advantages:

i. A rural or urban area is exclusively for one language which allows them to make decisions through their council meetings.
ii. Confinement of members to their own homeplace and land becoming a major language resource.

Limitations:

i. Tendency to partition into smaller nations.
ii. Non-interaction with outsiders leading to their own vision of the world.

5. Termination Model

Killing all people of other languages except one's own.

Advantages:

i.   Control of population explosion of other languages.
ii.   Improvement in one's own language identity.

Limitations:

i.   Violation of Right to life and personal liberty.
ii.   Increase in crimes like murder, execution, assassination etc.

WHICH MODEL IS CHOSEN BY INDIA?

India chose two models-Linguistic States Model and Linguistic Districts Model. Linguistic district model is used in states of North-East like Assam.

Eg:-Bodo language is a part of this model

Actually these two models are better than any other model.

SCOPE OF LINGUISTIC IDENTITY

The following are the incidents that happen to the people upholding his/her linguistic identity over other identities.

MERITS

i.   Translation of various texts into one's own language which gives more access to people.
ii.   Developing grammar and literature by writing stories, novels, drama, education book in one's own language.

DEMERITS

i.   Criticizes another linguistic identity that hurt the feelings of others which land him/her in jail
ii.   Difficulty in communicating and adjusting with other linguistic identity communities.

iii. Making friendship with those people only who speak their language either as mother tongue or second language.

LINGUISTIC MINORITIES

Those languages that are spoken by a very small population and included as Non-Scheduled language in the Constitution are linguistic minorities. These identities receive support from law in most countries but not from society. They are subjected to discrimination and if majority rules, minority identities demand the protection of their identity because they fear from the force and physical torture of majority. The Indian supreme law provide protection to them in Article 29 which states the right to preserve the language and script of minorities.

Linguistic minorities face the following challenges:-

i. No enough resource with them to increase the influence of their language through films or music.
ii. They are required to study majority's language for getting jobs or for doing education.
iii. Tends to lose many opportunities for success in life only because of lack of knowledge of majority language.

UNIQUENESS WITHIN LINGUISTIC IDENTITIES

Each person speak their own language which does not perfectly match with other. This feature is opposed by society by correcting the mistakes committed by person in language such as pronunciation. Actually, in order to maintain uniqueness in language, the languages should not be taught in schools and universities. At least, it should not be made compulsory. But this uniqueness is condemned as it may destroy a language and create personal language instead of group language which cannot be understood by the people belonging to same identity.

TYPES OF LINGUISTIC IDENTITIES

1.Spoken

It have words, sentences and talk between people only by using mouth.

2.Hand

The dumb people use the two hands for communication through the use of some symbols.

3.Secret Codes

This is used by intelligence officers or those who want to keep their language as 'known to only one additional person'. This is done in order to transfer information to another person without granting access to others.

PROBLEMS IN THE INTERIOR OF LINGUISTIC IDENTITIES

1) Abusive words and good words are unknown to identities against each other.

   Eg: 'A' may call bad word to 'B', which 'B' think that he got respect/dignity from 'A' if 'B' does not belong to linguistic identity of 'A' or is unaware of language spoken by 'A'.

2) The way of speaking may classify an identity as civilized or uncivilized.

Eg: A person speaking language in a simple manner and say wrong words in language may be considered as a person under or lower than a person who speak complicated language.

3) The language identity becomes consumed by cultural identity and this leads to common culture among a linguistic community. Eg: Tamil Culture.

LINGUISTIC INFLUENCES AMONG IDENTITIES

When one linguistic group is not aware of the thing or conditions of the outsider, the group would not have words related to the materials used by those outside their identity.

This will result in adoption of words from that linguistic identity outside to them. These are called linguistic influences. The consequences of these influences are:

i. A person belonging to one identity is able to understand the topic or at least the subject of the speech told by a person of another identity.

ii. There is only change in script and not in talk across linguistic identities.

iii. More developed countries uses hegemony in influencing other languages.

iv. As wealth of a country increases, the receive of linguistic influence decreases. It is because a country with more income may have large number of things which they have invented or discovered. They will coin the term and the countries with lower wealth just become followers.

LINGUISTIC IDENTITY OF A RULER

A King who uses the language of elites is considered as the ruler representing the richer and well-off categories. A King who uses the language of poor common ordinary man is considered as a 'welfare king'. Why is it so? If a King speak in the language of elites, the following are the effects:

(1)A common man can't understand his orders/laws that he described in speech or writing.

(2)People feel that the king is appointed or nominated by the elites and see king as oppressor and people living under suppression.

(3)Ordinary man have to approach a translator for talking to king which is difficult.

(4)People feels that king itself declared a language superior to those spoken by poor.

FEATURES OF MOTHER TONGUE

(1)   Mother Tongue can have three meanings:
    i.   The language spoken by mother.
    ii.   The language that a person spoke first after his birth.
    iii.   The language spoken by his whole family including cousins, relatives and distant connections or neighbours even though mother's language is different.

(2)   Mother Tongue is fixed and cannot be changed. This is rigid and denies the freedom of a person to alter or proudly claim that another language is his mother tongue. It is forced upon and one person loses his right to belong to different linguistic identity for

which he can become a victim of linguistic violence (only because of his mother tongue).

(3)   As father also plays an important role in choosing language of children, I suggest that it should be called 'Parent Tongue'.

CHAPTER-2

GENDER IDENTITY

NOTE

The author doesn't criticize any female identity or feminism. We request not to misunderstand this theory. He has only presented his views and does not intend to hurt anyone.

In this chapter we are discussing about the socio-economic and political scenario of gender identities.

CHANGING ROLE OF IDENTITIES

In the past, men go outside for work and women look after the household works. This is the organized structure of identities which is fixed by the society. The advantages of this organized structure of gender identities are:

i.   Increased specialization of work.
ii.   Division of duties and responsibilities within family which made a peaceful atmosphere.
iii.   No disguised labour and underemployment.
iv.   Ensuring strict separation between the genders in their professional and domestic spheres.
v.   Protection of women from the sexual abuse and harassment that happens outside their home.

The organised structure is breaking down year by year. It changed the overall society so rapidly in the urban areas that it caused many problems in the smooth functioning of society. They are as follows:

i.   The concept of 'Double Burden' emerged

- In the past, men did the office work and women was the manager of house. So, both were talented in each field and had successful family life. But now, women and men are doing the same work outside and inside. Even though their occupation may vary, internally, the pressure increases. Both men and women would only know about their occupation and may not know how to handle affairs of house. This may lead to household problems as they are unaware of the thing and situation in home.

ii.   Financial Expenditure increases

- The family have to appoint a servant or maid to clean the house, arrange it properly, wash clothes and do daily routines. Further, if the servant break anything in the house or cause a damage to it, the family will have to spend again to buy and restore the item. This happen when servant do not have adequate income to pay for damage and may instead prefer to leave job and look for another house. This adversely affect family as they will have to look for another maid.

iii.   Unhealthy habits arise within family

- As both parents go to work outside, the children may have to eat food from hotels and restaurants.
- They may consume junk food or the food with improper hygiene. This may make them to eat contaminated food which lead to food poison. The family may come back home at late night after work due to which child gets alone in the home. This may affect the psychological mindset of growing child that further lead to depression.

iv.   Conflicts within the family increase
- The males start to doubt females of their personal lives. The females also do many arguments against males that conflict become endless, and this may lead to divorce. When both husband and wife are doing work outside, their interaction among each other decrease and friends become more important than spouse for both of them.

v.   Women become vulnerable to crimes
- Women may face sexual assault, molestation and rape when they go outside for work. Similarly, there are many other issues which cannot be explained.

Some solutions should be found to tackle the above problems.

APPROACHES TO GENDER

1. Destructive

According to this approach, the gender justice means justice towards women only without considering justice towards men. This is an attempt to destroy the original meaning of the word gender to that of women only. For example, Sexual Harassment of Women at Workplace (Prevention, Prohibition and Redressal) Act, 2013 is a destructive approach which does not protect men from sexual harassment by women at workplaces.

2. Constructive

As per this approach, the gender justice is given to both men and women who are either victims or underprivileged. But this approach is not followed by a large majority of the countries including India. Though a partial constructive approach is taken by some Scandinavian and American countries, it is time for them to achieve a complete constructive approach to gender.

IDENTITY SUICIDE

An identity tries to improve but lands up in killing himself/herself. Identity suicides are increasing every decade. The factors responsible for identity suicide are:

i.   Technology innovations and advancement
ii.   Aims of uniformity
iii.   Acceptance of Cultural Hegemony
iv.   Desire to be like others, and not unique.
v.   Seeing another identity as model for one's own.
vi.   Adopting and practicing the lifestyle of other identity.
vii.   Hatred towards one's own identity

CONSEQUENCES OF IDENTITY SUICIDES

i.   The identity loses its value and significance.
ii.   The identity will be called a copy-pasted one.
iii.   The identity loses dignity and self-respect.
iv.   The identity accepts suppression and oppression from soft power techniques of other identity.
v.   Difficulty to identify an identity which makes identifiers to examine carefully or to ask their identity.
vi.   Those identity who didn't suicide feels alienation and sometimes anger against suicided identities. They automatically become minorities which increases identity discrimination.
vii.   The suicided identity, if take a second rebirth do not get recognized in society and society may

mock and tease the new born identity of the previous version.

viii. The suicided identity may take rebirth as a modified different identity such as the transgender category.

CONFLICT BETWEEN GENDER AND RELIGIOUS IDENTITIES

The feminist demanded that women should also get equal religious right in the famous Sabarimala temple which are given to men only by the prevalent customs. This demand was fulfilled by Supreme Court in 2018 Judgement. It told that women can enter the Sabarimala i.e. Lord Ayyappa temple which was restricted to women of reproductive age from 10 – 50 years since 1991 Kerala High Court rule. But this order of Supreme Court was based on the principle that it violates Article 14 of the Indian Constitution. Thus, women were allowed entry to the temple and Kerala State Government obeyed Supreme Court's decision. This hurt the Ayyappa devotees as women having menstrual cycle got entry. By this decision of Supreme Court, we can say that it violates Article 26 - Right to manage religious affairs. The devotees who have firm belief and faith in temple is not given a right to determine the laws of religion. Instead, an organ of government interfered unnecessarily only to favour women. This is the best example to show that we are losing the balance between gender and religious identity.

THE NEED FOR GENDER EQUALITY

There are cases where women throw acids on men's face and kill men. But men suffer as law do not take it seriously. The law enforcing agents consider only women as weak, marginalised, vulnerable and backward. They ignore men who are also there in same category. Some women tend to misuse the laws to maximum extent by false complaint against men in the court of law. Innocent men get punishment and even the society blindly believe women without investigations. The court delays the justice to men. All these creates gender inequalities.

UNFAIR LEGAL SUPPORT TO WOMEN

(1) The governments do not take into consideration the powerful women and give all protection to strong women too which enables some of these women to overexploit men.

(2) Certain terms such as healthy and positive sex ratio is biased in support of women. This means that if sex ratio increases so much, and males decline too great in number, then too sex ratio will be considered healthy because of more women.

(3) The provision of free legal aid to women affects the men as some women use free lawyers to target against men who have to pay for advocate.

(4) Government tends to focus more on women welfare than society's welfare leaving behind Scheduled Caste, Scheduled tribe and Other Backward Classes. Privileged women are getting more opportunities than lower caste men.

LUCKY WOMEN & UNLUCKY MEN

Giving away freebies to all women is actually a discriminatory practice. For example, a poor man has to pay bus charge while rich woman does not have to pay anything. The right way is to provide free service only to pregnant women or specially-abled women (facing disabilities)

TRANSGENDER EMPOWERMENT

There is a need to change from women empowerment to transgender empowerment. Women are already empowered by law and society, now it depends on the women's skill to come forward. But transgenders are largely discriminated even within their family. They face harassments and people consider them abnormal. All major official data sources in India provide sex related data only in male – female format which do not get contain transgender. Transgenders do not get adequate education facilities, medical treatment, employment (especially in bank services), homes, deprived of the entry to public places, and regarded them as outcaste and untouchable. It is their human right to lead a life with dignity and self – respect. But they are minorities and unable to participate in mainstream activities. We should have sympathy for transgender and help them in every situation.

TEACHING METHOD

In schools, it is taught that men make harsh and rash decisions while women are polite and are better leaders than men. These words unnecessarily praise one gender (female) at the cost of other gender (male). Thus, textbooks which teach this should be banned and teachers should teach both men and women can make good or bad decision based on one's character.

DOMESTIC VIOLENCE AGAINST MEN

This case happens in some households of India. Some women after becoming married, perform this domestic violence towards men where men suffer and do not get any relief from law. From one of the stories, I found the stages that lead to Domestic Violence as follows.

(1) Wife first tries to separate husband from his friends, relatives, cousins, brothers, sisters and parents.

(2) Wife starts to show over possessiveness and trap husband in all spheres of his life.

(3) She begins to quarrel and fight against husband for irrelevant reasons.

(4) She influences all his decisions and takes away his independence.

(5) She becomes angry for simple reasons and beats the husband with some things that are available immediately in place.

(6) The husband may be good, so he does not react and attempt to flee from his home. But husbands will be forced to stay due to marriage alliance.

The factors for this domestic violence are:

i. This domestic violence happens when wife has some other lover or is not interested in marriage but was forced by parents.

ii. Influence from television serials/web series or new films which focus on these themes.

FUTURE EXPECTATIONS AND PREDICTIONS

If we continue to follow 'Ladies First' principle, then in future, a matriarchal society can emerge where females become head of households, village, state and national government. A matrilineal lineage will also arise, and this is harmful. Accordingly, the following steps should be taken to avoid this situation.

i. A separate ministry and department on transgender empowerment should be made at Centre and States.

ii. Reservations should be given to transgenders for MP and MLA seats in Lok Sabha and State Legislative Assemblies according to their proportion of population.

iii. Either men's right ministry should be formed or ministry of women and child development should be changed to ministry of poor women and child development.

REFORMS TO GENDER INEQUALITY

(1) The law should provide reservations to only women belonging to Non-Creamy Layer that is those who are poor, backward, marginalized, deprived and lower castes. The rich and upper caste women should be excluded from the benefits of reservation and hence bringing gender equality.

(2) 'Ladies First' principle should be stopped and men and women should be always treated equal with special support for transgenders for next 25 years.

CHAPTER – 3

PROFESSIONAL IDENTITY

In this chapter, we discuss about different occupations of people and its identity impact on status both directly and indirectly.

FEATURES OF PROFESSIONAL IDENTITIES

(1) Determines class identity and family identity.
(2) A factor of superiority and inferiority identity.
(3) Responsible for formation of caste identity in the past.
(4) Formed by training and education in a specialized field of study.
(5) Occupational Inheritance was prevalent in past and now too on villages and slum colonies. This means that children take the same occupation of parents and follow their career.
(6) Occupational mobility is prevalent in metropolitan mega cities, towns, urban centers excluding family business. This means that children took different occupation not of their parents, or occupation do not pass across generations.

CLASSIFICATION OF PROFESSIONAL IDENTITIES

The professional identities may be broadly divided into ten (10) sub categories. They are:

(1) Religious professions.
(2) Governance and Administration profession.
(3) Business and trading professions.

(4) Management profession.
(5) Health Care Profession.
(6) Educational and Knowledge resource profession.
(7) Basic Amenity supplier profession.
(8) Comfort giving supplement profession.
(9) Technical profession.

(10) Political Profession.

RELIGIOUS PROFESSION

- It includes priest, bishop, monks, nuns, pope etc.
- Their workplace is a church, mosque, temple, or any other places of worship.
- Social and cultural identities play an important role in this profession.
- If a person belonging to religious professions became the head of the state, and establish his religion as official religion, then it is a theocratic state.
- Religious professions are denied to lower caste and people belonging to other religions. Women also do not have access to highest position in many religions.
- In Ancient India, only people belonging to Brahmana Varna, had the right to recite Vedas and do sacrifices on behalf of others.
- A person of religious profession establishes contact between God and other professional people.

GOVERNANCE AND ADMINISTRATIVE PROFESSION

- It includes civil servants/permanent executive, bureaucrats, district collectors, police, government employee.
- Some undertake the policy formation task with government and others its implementation.
- They give advice and recommendation to the government. They also draft bills and proposals.
- They are normally All – India Services, Central Service or State Service (Union Territories also) officers.
- Some of the examples of this professional job are of committees, commissions, NITI Aayog etc.
- They have a fixed post till retirement.
- They even evaluate and monitor policies.

BUSINESS AND TRADING PROFESSION

- It includes shopkeepers, merchants, big corporates, moneylenders, markets venders, street sellers etc.
- They make money for the sole motive of profit through bargaining and negotiating with consumers.
- They have a high dependence on customers.
- They may be wholesalers, retailers or intermediaries.
- They make the goods reach the purchasers from the point of production.
- They pay a huge amount of income tax and corporation tax for Central Government.

MANAGEMENT PROFESSION

- It includes the Human Resource Managers, accountants, bankers, entrepreneurs and decentralized heads.
- They do routine affairs of properly taking care of that company in a particular branch.
- They form a part of call centers and facilitate international commerce.
- They act as a bridge between the chairman of Company and the customers.
- They are paid salaries, and perhaps bonus.

HEALTH CARE PROFESSION

- It includes Doctors, Nurses, Health Workers and biologists.
- They treat the patients with the use of medicines. It can be Allopathy, Homeopathy, Ayurveda etc.
- They also give vaccines to population which prevents the spread of diseases and fever.
- This profession is one of the highest demanded at the service sector.

EDUCATION AND KNOWLEDGE RESOURCE PROFESSION

- This includes teachers, lecturers, professors and researchers.
- The specialist in subjects can be historians, economist, geographer, political theorist, sociologist, geologist, chemist, psychologist, physicist etc.
- They teach students or carry out data interpretation, field surveys and read and learn books.

- They are responsible for the creation of human capital and consequent human development.

BASIC AMENITY SUPPLIER PROFESSION

- They provide food such as those engaged in agricultural and allied sectors.
- They provide clothes for our wedding purposes.
- This profession includes cultivators, weavers, spinners, industrial workers, herders, pastoralist and those of all primary and secondary sectors.
- They are responsible for giving jobs to transporters, and majority of factory workers and tertiary sector people.

COMFORT GIVING SUPPLEMENT PROFESSION

- They sell luxurious and sometimes they are of low order also such as juice makers, hotels, restaurants, and what all work that people can do alone in their home without the help of others. These professions make the consumers lazy and their works become easy.

TECHNICAL PROFESSION

- It includes engineers, software developers, electronic operators etc.
- They are repairers or founders of new projects.
- They technically assist in all the jobs in hospitals, universities, government departments and IT sectors.

POLITICAL PROFESSION

- They include politicians, MPs, MLAs, (secretaries in case of US although not elected) and representatives of local bodies. The president is also having a political profession. The people working in this sector have only temporary job and losses their seat of power every 4 to 5 years which varies across countries. They can be thrown out from their profession easily by group of people.

CELEBRITY PROFESSION

These 10 professions are required for survival of human beings, and increase in standard of living. But there is another profession called celebrity profession which is just for entertainment purpose.

- It includes sports person, dances, singers, musicians, actors etc.
- They enjoy popularity among people.
- Income is directly proportional to their popularity.
- As popularity increases, income increases.
- But major criterion for popularity is skill and talents. Education is a minor or a not required criteria.

ILLEGAL PROFESSION

- Drug peddling, human trafficking, criminal actions are all declared as prohibited professions.

RIGHT TO FREEDOM OF PROFESSION, TRADE OR BUSINESS

- This right is included in article 19 (6) of the Constitution. This can be curtailed only when national emergency is declared on the grounds of external aggression or war. It is a fundamental right under part III and people can go to Supreme court or High court to restore this right.

PROFESSIONAL DISCRIMINATION

The lower order professions such as carpenters, barber, washerman, gardener, blacksmith and goldsmith are discriminated by upper order profession people like celebrity, business, and educational professions. The lower order workers get low income and bad working conditions. They may be even getting inadequate wages in some countries.

PROFESSIONAL DIVISION ACCORDING TO LOCATION

Geographical division of professions are usually seen in planned cities. Its main merit is that off reducing density of population, increasing cleanliness and hygiene and proper sizes of buildings seen around. Its demerit is that for instance, people belonging to educational area have to go far away to meet a health specialist which may even lead to death of sick person. That is, accessibility decrease with increasing geographical divisions of professions.

COOPERATION AND INTERLINKAGE OF PROFESSIONAL IDENTITIES

- Some professional identities are complementary to each other.
- In agriculture, farmers depend on fertilizers which is given by industry. Similarly, industries are dependent on farmers for raw materials. Similarly,

there should be friendship between producer and consumer for cooperation.

- If a producer of rice give rice to his friend who is a wheat producer, the wheat producer in turn give wheat back to rice producer. This encourages barter system and give and take policy.

ECONOMIC DIVISION OF PROFESSIONS

1) Primary- eg: Agriculture, fishing, domestication of animals.
2) Secondary- eg: manufacturing or industrial activities.
3) Tertiary- eg: doctors, teachers, lawyers, shopkeeper.
4) Quaternary – eg: R&D (Research and Development)
5) Quinary-eg: Highest level of decision makers.

PROFESSIONALISM

The competence or skill expected of a professional rather than being amateur is called professionalism. The large number of professional identities are illiterate and not properly trained. They lack skill and knowledge of the the profession they perform. Those who are highly talented go to foreign countries for getting job for getting higher income. What India should do is to make provisions for free training of professionals or if the budget becomes too high, at least the cost should be reduced and made cheaper or lend loans at low interest rate for professional training. Government can make incentives or make schemes for the purpose. Through this way, we can strengthen professionalism. Spread of awareness for the need of training can be also a measure.

REFORMS FOR PROFESSIONAL IDENTITY

1. By providing concessions and loans easily for those belonging to a particular profession, it can increase the demand for that profession.
2. Professional training can be imparted for school children from class 6 and facilitate it through digital platforms.
3. All unorganised sector workers should be taken into organised sector by creating more jobs in government services and consequently reducing unemployment.
4. All unorganised workers should be provided minimum protection at least from loss of jobs due to unfair reasons.
5. Parents should stop forcing children from following their profession and children should be given freedom to choose the profession of their interest and skill.

PRESENT SCENARIO

The society in North India mostly send their children to civil service and business management programs and South Indian society gives excessive value to science and technology, doctors, engineers and scientists.

PROFESSIONAL FAMILY DIVERSITY

If father is doctor, mother is engineer, elder son is teacher and younger son is civil servant while grandfather is Judge/Lawyer and grandmother is doing business by selling something, then the whole family is very powerful and becomes independent. It reduces their dependence on other family identities or outsiders. Thus, occupational mobility should be encouraged.

PROFESSIONAL ROLE MODELS

Some people can group together to perform one occupation if they are too deep friends or relatives. But first, one should take that profession and show others its advantages and disadvantages. This can make people think rationally on what profession is to be chosen.

PROFESSIONAL PROMOTION

One can promote their occupation to other people and be proud of it oneself so he/she can attract others to that profession.

PROFESSIONAL LEVELS

When one gets into a profession, on the first day he/she will be posted on junior/assistant level. Then after 3 or 5 years of experience, he/she may be promoted to next level which improves his/her identity and salary.

NON-RETIREMENT PROFESSIONS

Some professions such as doctors who practice privately and lawyers in some countries and businessman do not have retirement. He/she can practice the profession till death. This may be one of the reasons for increasing demand for these professions.

IDENTITY FAVOURED PROFESSIONS

This is the most dangerous one. Some heads of department in a job may choose those categories of people who belong to his/her identity. For example, if female candidates are only favoured by female employer or if one religion favours their own religious person over other religions.

CHAPTER-4
GENERATION IDENTITY

In this chapter, we are going to explore the identities of those who claim that they are new gen and those people who decide to remain as old generation.

DIFFERENCE BETWEEN OLD GENERATIONS AND NEW GENERATIONS

Old generation do not accept changes or they reject a new way of life while on the other hand, the new generations are those who adapt to technologies and latest inventions and discoveries which they use in day-to-day life. There are also some old generations who accept changes gradually or slowly and resist the rapid developments. They are called here conservative generations

OLD AND NEW GENERATION OF EARLY 20TH CENTURY

Here, we account for India's struggle to get independence from 1900-1947. Old generations did a violent form of protest against British rule such as killing of the officers and taking up arms. They follow the method of using weapons and muscle power. Here, old generation also includes young people who followed the old-styled procedure like that of Bhagat Singh in 1920s decade. The new generation started to do ahimsa and non-violence. Mahatma Gandhi is a new gen politically but an old gen technologically. He preferred handmade Khadi rather than machine made goods.

OLD AND NEW GENERATION OF 1950s AND 1960s

Old generation includes those who had fought the freedom struggle, those who favour centralisation and agriculturalist who do organic cultivation. The new generation aspire to work in industries, do agriculture with the use of green revolution and those who demand autonomy for States.

OLD AND NEW GENERATION OF 1970s AND 1980s

Old generation include those who accepted the supremacy of upper caste, those who desire to work on landholder's farm and who voted for National Party in state legislatures. New generation includes those Dalits who led a movement against untouchability, those who struggled to get rid of zamindari system and those who started to vote for regional political parties in federating units.

OLD AND NEW GENERATION OF 1990s AND 2000s

There occurred a wide gap between old and new generation. With the advent of LPG reforms (liberalisation, privatisation and globalisation) old and new generation splitted and kept away from each other. The old generation prefer public sector enterprises, import substitution and secondary or manufacturing sector development. The new generation prefer private investment and companies, greater exports of Indian products and imports of foreign products and a strong tertiary or service sector like IT (Information Technology). The computers began to be used popularly by the new generation. New generation also favour decentralization and local government.

OLD AND NEW GENERATION OF 2010s AND 2020s

Old generation includes male's rights advocate, emphasizes on Indian culture and strict marriage alliances between families. New generation included those who aspire westernisation, follow American or European model and extra Marital relationships. The new generation list also includes various use of gadgets, devices and electronic tools. The mobile (smart) phone addicts, online system of reading and playing are all examples of this new generation. The use of social media like Facebook, Twitter and WhatsApp are by the new generation users. Their mode of chatting and interacting is through video call platforms like zoom and Google meet. The new generation is exposed to radiation and eye stress which makes physical and psychological disorders and diseases. They have left connection with the environment where they live.

FEATURES OF GENERATIONAL IDENTITY

1) The generation gap strengthens Elderism. (For Knowing about Elderism please refer 'THE THEORY OF IDENTITIES: SOCIAL STRATIFICATION').

2) Generation influences culture and religion.

   Eg. New generation banned sati, child marriage and human sacrifice. Religion became more flexible.

3) A family identity is formed by generation gap.

4) The role of Identity such as gender change across generations. Society, economy,

technology and political identity are other examples for changes across generations.

5) Many diseases have become eliminated or rare across generations.
Eg. Smallpox (extinct)

6) Old generation can always visit the new generation and pass through it provided they don't die. But vice versa is not possible.

7) All new generations are convertible to become old generation after some years. For example, the new generation of 1950s are old generation of 2020s. Most of the new generations become rigid and start to follow strict social norms when they are converted after some years.

WHO ARE THE NEW GENERATION PEOPLE?

Those who are born after 1991 or those who are below 30 years of age and accept new style of Western clothing, fashion, craze, food habits and relationship are the new generation. Those who are young but don't accept it fall in the category of new born old generations. Those who are beyond the age or born before 1991 and accepted these new styles are modified-modernised old generation or called MM old gen.

RELATIONSHIP OF POLITICAL IDENTITY WITH GENERATIONAL IDENTITY

The parties of left front support old generation and right front supported new generation except their culture. Parties belonging to centralist ideology fully supported new generation as they are the ones who started liberalisation, privatization and globalisation. They had this relationship till early 2000s. Later all parties began to accept new generation like computers and laptops. Government is also aspiring to make digital India.

OLD GENERATION ATTITUDE VERSUS NEW GENERATION BEHAVIOUR

Old generation people were more attached to religion and hence they maintained some form of rules and regulations. They have trust and faith on their closed ones. They believe any story told to them. They don't distinguish between law and society and considered society as supreme law makers and not the government. They are rigid in character and very difficult to change them.

In contrast, new generation people are more rational and accept anything only if it have a scientific based evidence. They conduct enquiry and operation analysis or a data collection from any sources for believing any fact. They research and evaluate the society before giving up their thoughts. They consider Constitution as supreme law and government as their authority. They are very flexible and changes according to changing circumstances.

OLD GENERATION FILMS VS NEW GENERATION FILMS

Old generation movies have the following features:

    i.   Patriotism and Nationalism.
   ii.   Family relationship drama
  iii.   Romantic love stories.
  iv.   Entertainment and dream world.
   v.   Classical songs till late 1980s and modern classical till mid 2000s.

vi.   About 7 to 8 songs were there in one film with approximate 5 to 6 minutes for each.

vii.   Long duration often of three hours or 2hr 45 min.

New generation movies have the following features:

i.   Crime, thriller, mystery, suspense and spy. (Genre).

ii.   Drugs, alcohol, cigarette smoking.

iii.   Violence and investigation types.

iv.   Very less songs or no song at all.

v.   Short duration of 1hr 30min or 2hr

vi.   Corruption, smuggling, and politics are the main themes.

NEW GENERATION IMPACT ON MUSIC

New generation changed the old music structure which used to be like 'Hey Hey, Ha Ha, Oh Oh, La La'. It reduced the in depth meaning of poems also. Lyricist begin to be side lined by music directors. It lost its melodious character.

BUILDING GENERATIONS

Generations can go forward only by reproduction. Emphasizes on contraceptives may lead to decrease in fertility rate and improvement in health care can lead to an increase in life expectancy. This can increase the population of old generation, thereby increasing the influence. 'One – child policy' is an initiative for reducing new generations.

GENERATIONAL DOWNGRADE

Afghanistan which had a high improvement in education and employment during 1920s have fallen in late 1990s and early 2000s during Taliban rule. This shows what happens when democracy get transition to dictatorship.

GENERATIONAL PSYCHOLOGY

New generations of younger age aspire for becoming elder and elder.

1. A school child wishes to grow fast to be able to go to college.
2. A college student desire to get married as soon as possible and get children.
3. A married man and father after getting job wishes to become old, so that he can rest.

Old generations aspire for becoming younger and younger.

1. Old aged people due to sickness and health problems remembers his childhood or college days or a good married life. He things that he has lost his energetic age where he could enjoy with his friends.
2. Some middle aged aspires to go back to his past and become a baby or a kid and always get pampering.

GENERATIONAL MEDIA

Drawing, Painting, Writing or any form of artistic activity may spread across new generations for thousands of years if it is considered valuable.

E.g.: Bhimbetka Cave Paintings.

Similarly, one's good actions are always inspired by new generations even after one's death.

Eg:-Mahatma Gandhi(Father of Indian Nation)

Sardar Vallabhbhai Patel (Ironman of India)

PERFECT GENERATIONAL IDENTITY

When one generational identity contributes much to the world or national progress by making a lot of developments in various fields such as commerce,literature,heritage,coin minting,technology,architecture,language,subjcts of study and military etc, it gets a perfect status of 'Golden Age'

Eg:-Gupta Period.

This generation is known for remarkable achievements.

GENERATIONAL NUMBER

Many electronics are named as 1st generation,2nd generation etc depending on its more development and launch date.

DENSITY OF GENERATIONAL IDENTITY

Niger has the largest upcoming new generation (50%) why Japan has the largest old generation (27%). Working age of people till 32 years are new generation and above that is old generation.

$$N_D = \frac{T_{GI} - O_{GI}}{T_{GI}} \times 100$$

$$O_D = \frac{T_{GI} - N_{GI}}{T_{GI}} \times 100$$

Here: N_D is new generation density.

O_D is old generation density

T_{GI} is total generation Identity

N_{GI} is New generation Identity

O_{GI} is Old generation Identity

Eg. Total population of place A is 600

Old generation =200.

$$N_D = \frac{T_{GI} - O_{DI}}{T_{GI}} \times 100 = \frac{600 - 200}{600} \times 100$$

$$= \frac{400}{600} \times 100 = \frac{400}{6} \times 1$$

$$= 66.66\% \text{ of new generation.}$$

This explains that when the amount of new generation increased beyond 50%, the country will have a high degree of new gen influence and governments are the representatives of new generation majority if the people from 18 to 32 years are greater in number than those beyond 32.

GENERATIONAL INHERITANCE

New generation who occupy the old generation's property for long years and continues again across generations become zamindars and landlords. Similarly, the son accedes to the throne of the king with this characteristic of generational inheritance. The generational inheritance faced challenges after India declared its independence. They are:-

1. Democracy and Republican form of government.
2. Land reforms and land ceiling act.

The generational inheritance continue in some countries with constitutional monarchy such as United Kingdom.

FUTURE PROSPECTS OF OLD AND NEW GENERATION

Old generation may stick to social norms initially but will decline. Old generation may convert to new generation category. New generation will depend more on science and robots including voice assistant such as Amazon Alexa, Google home or Apple Siri. New generation may reduce the beliefs in mythologies and start searching for reality and truth. The new generations are likely to take jobs in quaternary and quinary sector. There is a chance for more cyber wars and its protection schemes taken by government. International cooperation can increase and World governments may be formed. Sustainable development would be the focus of new generation and more fundamental rights will get interpretation from Supreme court. Digitalisation may increase and new identities can evolve in few years.

CHAPTER-5

HISTORICAL IDENTITY

In this chapter, we discuss how our identities were shaped in the past and how we reacted to the identities assigned to us.

FUNDAMENTAL DIFFERENCE BETWEEN MONARCHY AND DEMOCRACY

1. People are subjects of a ruler in monarchy while they are citizens of a nation in democracy.
2. Most of the identities of people are determined by the king in monarchy while people get freedom to decide their all identities except those fixed by the nature in a democracy.
3. People's Identities are under threat in a monarchy while it is safe and secure in democracy.
4. People usually gets discriminatory identities from society if the monarchy supported brahmanism while in democracy, as people elect their rulers, they are more likely to get identities on equality basis.

IDENTITY SYSTEM IN DICTATORSHIP ESPECIALLY THAT OF MILITARY

1. The top of the triangle consists of dictator and just bottom of it his agents of service. They favour their own identity and may try to eliminate other identities or may put them in prison.
   Eg. Adolf Hitler killed a large number of Jews and supported 'German Aryans'.
2. A total breakdown of Identity system and its destruction in such a way that it may get difficulty to

revive. But the law of returning identity prevails, so the Identity may slowly get back to its position at least in a different place.

Eg. Jews who enjoyed their life during Weimer republic were destroyed during Nazi Regime and after the end of Nazis also, so many Jews had to protest for homeland, 'Palestine' which was occupied by Arabs because Jews were driven out during Roman empire's rule. Then after the formation of Israel, Jews became one of the best contributors in technology and military.

IDENTITIES OF ANCIENT INDIA

1. Caste Identity

    In ancient India, Buddhist and Jains have considerably improved their identity with a lot of grants that they received from rulers. Kshatriyas, the warrior class have improved their political identity. Vaishyas, the peasants and traders improve their economic identity and shudras improve their social identity during this period by joining Buddhism and Jainism.

    Brahmanas enjoyed a high status of Identity as they had the sole rights in all religious and cultural affairs. They recited Vedas, performed sacrifices and did rituals. They were the most literate identity.

2. Linguistic Identity

    Linguistic identities such as Prakrit got boosted in Jainism and Pali got prominence under Buddhism. Sanskrit became the medium for Hinduism. Literature for each identity was developed.

3. Gender Identity

During Rig Vedic period, women had a better identity of being able to attend Vedic assemblies and there was no Sati. There was no child marriage and women got opportunities for spiritual and intellectual development. There were women poets also. Women like Prabhavati Gupta efficiently ruled the Vakataka kingdom for 20 years.

4. Class Identity

With the circulation of gold coins and facilitation of trade, the empires became prosperous and many Vaishyas turn out to be wealthy.

5. Educational Identity

The Nalanda University and Vikramsila University made many scholars at that time. Aryabhatta, a famous astronomer had one of the highest education identity.

6. Age Identity

Ashoka's Dhamma policy which told respect towards elders have further improved age identity.

IDENTITIES OF MEDIEVAL INDIA

1. Religious Identity

New religion appeared in Indian subcontinent such as that of Islam and Sikhism. The sufis came to India with the concept of deep devotion and Mysticism.

2. Political Identity

This period saw the entry of invaders like Sultanate (both Delhi and Decan) and Mughal Empire. The Vijayanagara empire formed in South India. Maharana Pratap in Mewar region maintained a secular Kingdom. Shivaji's Maratha empire developed during this time.

3. Economic Identity

Connections with Central Asia and middle East especially countries like Persia give a different economic identity to people. Many travellers such as Ibn Battuta and Francis Bernier came to India during this time and evaluated the economic Identity of India.

IDENTITIES IN MUGHAL EMPIRE

Lower-level identities.

1. Majur-Menials or agricultural labourers
2. Halalkhoran-Muslim communities menials.
3. Mallahzadas-sons of boatmen.
4. Jats
   - Tribals had the most depressed identity.

Middle-level identities

1) Gauravas-cultivated land around Vrindavan.
2) Ahirs.
3) Gujars — Profitability of cattle rearing & horticulture
4) Malis
   - Sadgops and Kaivartas (fishing caste) acquired the status of peasants.

Upper-level identities

1) Patwari - accountant
2) Mandal or Muqaddam (headman of village)
3) Imams
4) Brahmins
   - Mughal emperor was at the top of hierarchy. The identity of first six great Mughal emperors such as Babur, Humayun, Akbar, Jahangir, Shah Jahan and Aurangzeb were too much better than the later emperors.

IDENTITIES OF MODERN INDIA

The identities were modernized during this period with Indians coming across many technologies. The Portuguese, French, Dutch and other foreigners entered India.

BRITISH MODEL OF CREATING IDENTITIES

1) **Indirect rule in the princely states.**
   The people in 565 princely states were ruled by their princes. The prince had to obey the paramount British. The autonomy of Prince was severely affected.
2) **Integration with Indian identities**
   British brought their Western institutions, schooling and promoted Christianity religion and integrated with the Indian identities. Currently, India have Western type of recognised schooling and adopted parliamentary form of Government from British. India has more than 2% of Christianity with some States having its majority. Thus, British brought a new education identity and increased the population of one religious identity.

3) Mixed identity effect

Some identities such as economic identities, social identities, class identities and caste identities have collapsed under British rule but gender identity and technological identity except agriculture has improved.

Eg. The starting of railways

IDENTITY DEFECTION

During British rule, many people defected to Christianity for protection from evils of their religion and also due to force by foreigners. Some people also defected from National identity to serve the British army. As the defection increased, the struggle for independence increased to stop this identity defection. Identity defection is not new. In ancient India, Kushans and Shakas have defected their outcaste identity to belong to second class Kshatriya. Even Hindus converted to Buddhism and Jainism during this period. Difference between Identity Defection and identity flow is that identity Defection does not involve second person's role of propagation. The defection is to escape from something. It has a motive. But identity flow do not have necessarily a motive. It is once own wish after somebody has propagated him about it. Identity Defection is also different from identity tour as defection is not for test or do not come back to previous identity by regret. Here, Defection is permanent and may change to another identity but not the original or previous identity.

SATISFACTION WITH HISTORICAL IDENTITIES

Some people are not satisfied with their past identities such as regional identity. They demanded the formation of linguistic states in 1950s. Therefore, the administrative Provinces were changed to linguistic States. Some people are not satisfied with their past local identity. It is because their local area is incapable of providing employment, for healthcare and for education that they forgo their historical identity and makes a new identity by permanently migrating to a different area. Again, those who are not satisfied with their class identity in which historically they were poor, they transform identity by doing higher education or conducting a profitable business.

FEATURES OF HISTORICAL IDENTITY

i.   Historical identity fixes an identity of a person at his birth without his consent.

ii. Some historical identities are changeable while others are not.
     Eg. Class, local and regional identity is changeable.
     Caste, human and family identity is unchangeable.

iii. Historical identities cannot be traced back beyond 500 years by any single family. Some ancient and medieval identities remain unknown.

iv. Historical identities have strong relationship with political, social, economic and locational identities.

HISTORICAL IDENTITIES OF EUROPE

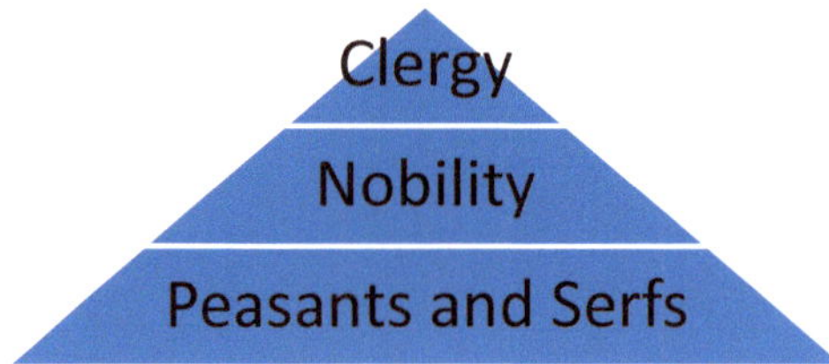

These were the three orders which were called Three estates in France.

The church had occupied the peak of identities. The most influential and powerful identity was the priest. The Clergy included bishop, clerics, etc. The head of Western Church was pope. He had high class identity because of money given in the form of endowments by rich. They were included in the top economic identity as they were entitled to a tenth share of produce of peasants.

The nobility is the identity of landowners who are vassals of the king. Unlike Clergy who have an independent identity, nobles had their identity attached with the king. They had absolute control over property and owned large sums of estates. They had a high status in political identity as they could coin their money and raise troops. They had a privileged legal identity as they hold their own courts of justice.

The cultivators had the lowermost Identity. The free peasants render military service, unpaid service and have to pay taxes to King also. They had a depressed class identity and suffered in their economic identity. On the other hand, Serfs did not had a a good political identity because they did not enjoy freedom. Their political identity was at the mercy of 'Lord'. Serfs could not leave the estate without lord's permission and lord decided whom they should marry.

CRITICISMS OF HISTORICAL IDENTITY

i. Historical identity does not have a valid proof except that of evidence collected from inscriptions, coins, archaeology, foreign accounts and other sources. No one in the present have seen the past and these historical identities are constructed by intelligence and beliefs.

ii.   Historical identities take an identity researcher to the subject of history that gets overlapped with the work of a historian. It makes an inter - disciplinary conflict.

iii. Historical identity may have changed over a period of time. So, there is no single identity of a person or group that we can study. The next generation might had a completely different identity.
Eg. Mauryan identities are not Mughal identities.

iv.   Historical identities become a factor for a current identity's pride and honour. It can have both positive and negative effects. If historical identity gets out to be a good one, that identity becomes proud. While the current identity's dignity decreases when historical identity reveals to be bad.

v.   Historical identities are misinterpreted regularly by different religious identities which gets injected into society that makes conflicts. Some examples are saffronization and Islamization.

REFORMS FOR HISTORICAL IDENTITY

I.   People should not develop a spirit in historical identity with full faith. It should be only moderate.

II.   Historical identity studies shall be separated from the work of a historian and given to identity researches. But historian can assist the work with identity researchers.

III. The school and college academic textbook should be made secular and only truth shall be revealed.

IV.   All the sources of history shall be made available for identity researchers and identities should be reconstructed through puzzle match method. That is all piece-to-piece construction of identities from different sources should be done so that the identities of people get separated from different topics in history such as economy and society of Empire.

V. There should be a complete ban on religious identity's interference in historical identities. They should not be allowed to make historical identities their puppet.

CHAPTER – 6

STEREOTYPE WITH IDENTITY

Even though stereotype is not an identity, here we are saying about the stereotype that exists between identities. In this chapter, we discuss about a person's oversimplified image of an identity. Stereotype is an idea of a particular type of person or thing. It is widely held and fixed. It is a part of rainbow of discriminatory identities in the sense that this is a factor for discrimination between identities. This is the smallest chapter.

CAUSES OF STEREOTYPE WITH IDENTITY

I. Inter-community conflicts, tensions and violence.
II. Communal clashes and further disintegration.
III. Feeling of suspicion and distrust.
IV. Notion that identities are having opposed interests and sharply defined boundaries.
V. The concept of "one person are all persons". That is thinking the one individual as the model or representative of whole group.
VI. Maintaining foes and enemies.
VII. Identity spirit and dream of 'one place, one identity' which is the impossible dream.
VIII. Cultural beliefs and social discrimination.
IX. Prejudice and non-rational viewpoints.
X. Sometimes done to prevent interactions.

CONSEQUENCES OF STEREOTYPE WITH IDENTITIES

i. Separation and keeping away from each other.

ii.   Misunderstanding and wrong knowledge for upcoming generations which leads to alienation of group.

iii.   Non-cooperation with other identities strengthens division of society. It creates barrier in communication.

iv.   Secession of a territory.

STEREOTYPE PROCESS

I.   One identity may be stereotyped at the time when only one person belonging to that identity make some issues or problems. Because of one person, the whole group belonging to that identity get stereotyped.

II.   If first identity have a high density of population of the category of a single feature in a particular area, the other people of this area may observe the first identity's whole people across the world in a similar way.
Eg. If lower caste in place A is having high density of population and they are 'dark' in colour, the upper caste of place 'A' may feel that lower caste around the World is dark provided that he/she is not highly educated. Thus, he/she stereotypes an identity.

III.   If one identity stereotypes another identity, by law of reflecting discrimination, identity get stereotyped back.

STEREOTYPE MEDIA

i.   White talking with friends or family.

ii.   Through social media which has decreased over the years because this has welcomed many people to prisons.

iii.   Direct speech towards an identity with stereotype-related content.

iv.   Arts like drawing, painting, comics and cartoon.

IDENTITY PSYCHOLOGY AND ACTION ON BEING STEREOTYPED

i.   A feeling of insult and crave for revenge.

ii.   Cursing another identity for doing stereotypes.

iii.   Arguments and consequent fighting.

iv.   Appeal to legal system and administrators.

v.   A group protest, demonstrations and movement.

vi.   Raising questions on stereotype.

vii.   Breaking alliances and inter-identity marriages.

POSITIVE STEREOTYPING OF IDENTITY

Sometimes an identity stereotypes other identity as calm, good, kind and godly which actually may be bad. This result in some problems with stereo typist.

Eg. Group of robbers may be having a different image in society as they disguise themselves at different times. The society may regard them as good without knowing that they are great robbers.

WHAT DIFFERENT APPROACH?

Stereotypes can be two-explicit and implicit. But we are not discussing it here because the stereotype completely belongs to sociology and psychology. And there is nothing to deal extra in identity science. Similarly, the models of stereotype content, functions of stereotypes, role and posters are not going to be explained. On different perspective, let's go to next topic.

RELATIONSHIP BETWEEN PEOPLE'S IDENTITY AND STEREOTYPE

i.   **Class Identity Stereotype**

A rich person can stereotype a poor on hygiene, cleanliness, nature of character etc. Similarly, a poor person can stereotype rich on greediness, corruption and attitude.

ii. **Caste Identity Stereotype**

An upper caste may stereotype a lower caste and vice versa.

iii. **Gender Identity Stereotypes**

Female may stereotype males or vice-versa. Or one of them may stereotype transgenders or vice-versa.

iv. **Linguistic Identity Stereotype**

An urban community may stereotype the tribal people based on language they speak.

v.   **Superiority Identity Stereotype**

The category of people who is seen as inferior by superior may be stereotyped.

vi. **Age and Family Identity Stereotype**

These stereotype have very little chance of accuracy.

vii. **Generational Identity Stereotype**

Usually, old generation stereotype new generation as drug addicts, flirt and non-advisable behaviour.

viii. **Historical Identity Stereotype**

This has intimate connection with religious identity.

ix. **Professional Identity stereotype**

Doctors are not seen as human beings and are ill-treated by some identities.

CHAPTER– 7

SINGLE PERSON IDENTITY

In this chapter, we discuss about the identity of one individual instead of focusing on a group. An individual is also a member of group identity such as his/her caste, class, religion, gender, age, family, majority/minority, race, language, profession etc. But he/she is also so different from others in a group.

FEATURES OF SINGLE PERSON'S IDENTITY

1. Uniqueness of Identity that does not resemble others.
2. Determined by his/her desires, wishes, ambitions, goals etc.
3. One's ability, capability, skills and talents play an important role in deciding one's own identity.
4. Many persons may have same name, but the way of distinguishing them is through the application of single Person's identity. For this, a person's name, age, profession/student, address, father's name, etc would be used to differentiate between persons. This means that single Person's identity is dependent on group identity.

IDENTITY CYCLE

Some persons may wish to get rid of cycle in which they are the born again in earth to suffer from identities. Thus, they do a lot of sacrifice in their life. Here, sacrifice does not mean killing animals. It means that he/she is sacrificing himself/herself. They may do meditation, goes to search for truth and stay away from luxuries. When they get enlightenment, they get free from this identity cycle. The religion, Buddhism and Jainism aims to get out of the cycle of Karma and get the Nirvana. It is similar to getting rid of an identity cycle even though the aim of this enlightenment is different.

ELEMENTS OF IDENTITY IMPROVEMENT

The elements of identity improvement helps in improving a depressed identity from the position of being suppressed. These elements include:-

1   Education
2   Professional training
3   Doing a successful business
4   Good social work
5   Getting elected to legislature

there should be reservation for depressed identity in order to get benefit from the elements of Identity improvement in entry (1), (2) and (5). Legal support and financial aid are required for elements of Identity improvement in (3) and (4).

TYPES OF SINGLE PERSON'S IDENTITY APPOROACH

1. Equa- Identity Approach
    A single person having equa-identity approach gives equal value to his/her all identities without giving any excessive spirit to one identity. This is the most favorable approach as it does not lead to identity conflicts.

2. Zero-Identity Approach
    A single person who does not give any value to all his/her identities and even is happy to hear criticisms

about his/her identities. This is rare but this approach is a self suicide approach and does not harm others.

3. One- Identity Approach

A single person gives value to only one identity and other identities are shadowed. This means that a person's whole spirit is on one identity and this makes inter-identity conflicts.

4. Situational Identity Approach

A person gives value to his/her identity on the basis of his mood which changes with time and day. Situational identity approach is very dangerous as another person before saying anything about the first person's identity may not know his mood. This may lead to sudden reaction and inter-identity conflicts.

5. Max-identity Approach

A person may give value to maximum number of identities that he/she have. One identity may be excluded. The excluded identity may degrade and included identities may become conservative in future.

6. No-group Identity Approach

A person may consider himself independent of all group identities even if it is impossible. He may try to create his own idea of identities such as new religion, new language etc. He may be the only follower of his idea and thus inter-identity conflicts arises between him and his family or close relatives. He may be also expelled from his family that strengthens No-group Identity Approach. He then struggles to live alone in this complex world.

7. Location based Identity Approach.

A person's spirit for identity changes with place. When he is at home, he gives importance to family identity; at temple/church/mosque he gives importance to religious identity; at office, he gives importance to professional identity. This is a planned identity approach to follow all disciplines.

8. Behalf-Identity Approach

    Some people show spirit for the identity of wife, children, grandchildren, parents and grandparents. He may consider his own identity as below them.

BIOLOGICAL IDENTITIES FOR A SINGLE PERSON

DNA test and gene tracing can be adopted for having a person's biological identity. Marks on the body, structure and colour can be also a factor for creation of biological identities.

GEOGRAPHICAL AGENDA OF IDENTITIES

1) National Identity

    A single person may be proud of his nation and praise it in all the spheres of his life. He respects the National Flag, National Anthem and is very patriotic. He favours more power to Central Government or Union Government than the States. He have deep dignity towards the nation's constitution and may serve in military defence or represents his nation in international organization. He is willing for a unitary system than for federalism.

2) Regionalist Identity

    A person may ask more autonomy for his region from the Centre. He may be involved in inter-state conflicts and may take state emblem as his emblem. He represents state at National level meetings and give more importance to the identity of the state on which it divided. As India is having Linguistic States, for instance a person from Maharashtra may give spirit to regional identity. When the spirit of regionalism exceeds a limit, it becomes regionalist nationalism demanding the formation of separate nation for one identity.

3) Local Identity

A person may be attached to his District or village where he is born or residing since his birth. He desires for a decentralized government with Panchayats and Corporations getting enough powers and financial resources.

4) Universal Identity

A person may wish to get a universal citizenship so that he doesn't want a VISA or will not have to stay as refugees.

GLOBAL IDENTITY FOR ALL INDIVIDUALS

With the spread of internet, a single person's identity get connections with all persons across the world. He gets opportunity to communicate with people in different parts of the world through social media. His individual identity get improved and do not have to depend on others. He can import any products from different country through international online shopping. He can know what is happening in another continent through T.V News and Newspapers. Radio is also connected with information of international importance. Struggle to identify life outside Earth enhance a global identity for an individual. With New Economic Policy of 1991, Liberalisation, Privatisation and Globalisation started in India which led to a steady improvement in global identity at higher rates. Global identity became a single person's identity from the status of a group identity.

SPORTSMAN SPIRIT IN AN INDIVIDUAL IDENTITY

When one person wins a match in a game, he/she develops a winner identity. Those who get defeated adopts a loser identity. Law of returning Identities work in this situation to uplift the loser identity to a position of winner's identity at least in a different game. But law of returning identities requires a sportsman spirit of the person in order to work effectively. Otherwise, the law gets paused.

GOVERNMENT GIVEN IDENTITIES FOR AN INDIVIDUAL

- Aadhar card
- Voter ID Card
- PAN Card
- Driving License (if person gets license)
- Digital ID such as Health Card
- Birth Certificate
- Educational certificate (if he pursues studies in recognized school or college/university)

If government gives identities to the people, it would be combined with rights or duties/responsibilities. These 10 cards are necessary for every important task in life especially one is required for updating other.

INDIVIDUAL GIVEN IDENTITIES FOR GOVERNMENT

- ❖ Support in elections and trust.

- ❖ Transferring power to a small group.
- ❖ Opportunities to government for carrying out policies.

Even though the above three are not identities, these three are the factors for that give identity to government.

- A feature of Individual given identities to government is that they can take this identity back or delete this identity at any time if they have support of group of individuals. But Government given identity is non-transferable and it is permanent for an individual. His death identity card is made by his family members after his death. This is popularly referred to as Death Certificate.

INDIVIDUAL IDENTITY'S PERSONALITY DEVELOPMENT

The Fundamental Rights especially Article 19 in Part III of Indian Constitution give six basic rights to an individual identity for the development of Personality with some limitations. The civil liberties and political rights are the way for developments of single person's personality. The identity improves with Freedoms of Speech and Expression (Article $19_{(1)}$), Freedom of Press (also in Article 19 with wider interpretation), Freedom to assemble peacefully without arms (Article $19_{(2)}$), Freedom to form associations and trade unions (Article $19_{(3)}$), freedom to move throughout the country (Article $19_{(4)}$), freedom to reside and settle in any part of the country (Article $19_{(5)}$). The Article $19_{(6)}$ is best for professional identities which is also good for personality development of an identity.

PUSH-PULL FACTORS FOR IDENTITY DEVELOPMENT

A single person's identity is pushed forward by the following factors:-

- Legal Support
- Excitement in subconscious mind for developing own identity.
- Self-reliant and having self-esteem.
- Ready to adjust with prevailing majority's environment.
- Following the ideals of peace.

A single person's identity is pulled backwards by the following factors:-

- Loss of self-confidence and diversion from development.
- Conservative pullback from society and distractions.
- Lack of energy and infrastructure.
- Going behind shortcuts instead of being straight forward.
- External agency's influence. The example of this are bad advices, mocking, teasing etc which changes the decision of identity developer.

IDENTITY EFFECTS ON AN INDIVIDUAL

As one forms a part of group identity, the majority's actions affect a single person's identity personally also. For example, Person A is working in a company where majority do corruption. So, Person 'A' will be considered by the society as the person who do corruption. Also, Police may call him for questioning due to suspicions. That is why, it is said to good persons not to make any friendship with robbers.

CHALLENGES TO SINGLE PERSON'S IDENTITY

- As single person's identity is very narrow and do not enjoy broad acceptance, it can be wiped out fastly and a person may become like other person due to force from society.
- The main threat to a single person's identity is from his dear ones like parents, siblings, teachers, spouse etc. Eg. Wife ask a husband to become like other husbands or teachers ask students to become like the topper of class. (Reference: 'I Will Fly' by APJ Abdul Kalam.
- A person not having a strong determination power and is too flexible do self-destruction of Identity.
- The principle of 'equality' brings a huge challenge to single person's identity with expanding interpretations. Positively, equality give equal punishment for offenders belonging to any identity. On the other side, if merit is not considered and given equality, it negatively affects a person's identity.

NEW SCOPE OF IDENTITY

In early years, a single person associated his identity with locational, social, economic, political and historical identity. Now, technological identities like Email ID and mobile number became a single person's identity. Before, Telephone number was for a group identity. But now, as everyone have their own phone, it became a single person's identity. Also, initially when WhatsApp released, people used their mobile numbers for the app. Later, due to overloading of messages people started to separate mobile numbers into two-one for calling and other for WhatsApp. So, WhatsApp number became a single person's identity. Emerging fields like e-tech, e-governance and e-learning can facilitate the creation of new identities. These can be called Electronically Generated Identities. Digital literacy is a new criterion for determining an identity as a literate or not.

COVID-19 IMPACTS ON IDENTITIES

In December 2019, COVID-19 broke out in China and it came to India in January 2020. By February, all South Indian states along with West India got many cases of COVID-19. It spread to North India and east India in March which led Government of India to impose lockdown nationwide on March 23 which continued till May 31 2020. In the four lockdowns, Lakshadweep, a Union Territory had no reported cases. Then, from June month onwards, States began to impose lockdowns by finding hotspots. These Lockdowns had the following impact on identities.

- **An Alteration In Class Identity**
  Those rich people who had improved their identity using business have depressed it during lockdown as business failed.

- **Deterioration In Economic Identity**
  The poor people lost their livelihood and income during lockdowns.

- **Locational Identity Under Stress**
  Those who had migrated for work became unemployed during lockdown and wish to go back to home to see their family. But as transportation stopped their service and Airways suspended flights,

people found it difficult to go back. Some walked to house while other stayed there.

- Improvement In Human Identity

  The lockdown could protect many people from pandemic and in this way many people got good health and improved their human identity.

- Improvement In Living Being Identity

  Environment became free from pollution to most extent as vehicles were very less on road due to border controls and thus plants and trees could live peacefully. Animals could breathe fresh air as many industries shut down and some opened only alternate days.

DID PEOPLE TRY TO PROTECT THEIR IDENTITIES DURING PANDEMIC BY THEMSELVES?

The answer is that majority did not try to protect themselves. Here 'identity' in pandemic is all about 'living' and 'health' identity. Many people converted their identity to 'diseased identity' by not following COVID protocols. It is proved below:-

- Not Wearing Mask Properly

  Some people do not even have masks. Many others have mask but they put it on beard and do not close their nose with mask.

  Reasons

  - Over-confidence that they will not get COVID-19. There is a belief that people are unable to hear when one speaks inside mask.
  - People say that they are unable to breathe well by wearing mask. (This is not an excuse)

> ➢ People claim that mask automatically go down and they are tired of putting it up.
> ➢ There is a widespread belief that relatives, cousins and friends do not have COVID-19.

- Not Sanitizing Hands

Some people do not buy sanitizer while many others buy but do not use.

Reasons

> ➢ Poor people argue that sanitizers are costly.
> ➢ Old people say that sanitizers are cold or they are having bad smell that they can't tolerate it.
> ➢ Some people say that they forget to take sanitizers from home.

- Not Maintaining Social Distancing Of 2 Meters

Reasons

> ➢ Some people do not know calculation for measurement as they say 0.5 m as more than 2 m.
> ➢ People go and eat in the hotels by removing mask and server comes so near to the customer by saying that it's the duty to serve the customer and to properly hear orders. Customers don't take parcel as majority are lazy to clean plates or don't directly go to home.

POST COVID-19 IDENTITIES

With the arrival of second dose vaccinations in India such as COVAXIN and COVISHIELD, the people develop new belief that after vaccination, they will be never infected with COVID-19. This belief even spread to those highly educated researches and college lecturers. US government approved

Pfizer for their population. Similarly, many European countries have taken vaccination. This created new identity division on the basis of vaccination taken. For example, those who didn't take vaccination are not allowed to enter some shop's premises or University campus. Even those who took only one dose are discriminated in the form of modern untouchability.

Actually, those who don't wear mask, sanitize hands and don't follow social distancing should be restricted access to public places rather than those who only didn't vaccinate but followed all other protocols. It should be done in this manner so that people start to follow wearing mask appropriately and maintain social distancing. This is the reform that has to be taken. There are instances of people getting COVID-19 for 2nd time or getting it even after vaccination. But the psychology of ordinary people do not bother it and think it as fake news. Thus, it leads to high mortality and never-ending cases.

The lawmakers and the government are not following covid-19 protocols personally, then how citizens will follow? Thus, it is necessary that a top official or a popular celebrity follow strict protocols and become a model for the people. Post-COVID identities should be protected collectively rather than by individual single person's effort.

An individual's identity does not have capability of being protected without the involvement of group in the case of pandemic like COVID-19. It has taught a lesson that an individual exists only if group accept his existence.

IDEOLOGICAL DIFFERENCES BETWEEN SAME IDENTITIES

One may be a Nationalist, socialist, advocate of equality and men's right supporter. While another person belonging to the same identity of first person may be a regionalist, advocate of privilege and feminist. That is to say, ideologies differ from one person to another.

STANDARD AND PREMIUM IDENTITIES

The identities that are being taken freely or willingly are standard identities while those identities that are taken after being paid are premium identities. The examples of premium identities are mentioned below:

Eg. Some people get converted to other religion by getting money from a person of other religion. Some people may migrate to another place and leave home because of getting a lot of cash and coins. Some people are being paid to say criticisms against their own identity.

LOVE IDENTITY

For a single person's identity, the more serious sub-classified identity is love identity. A person may be a 'lover' of someone or he/she love someone and make that person a 'lover'. In this context, we are dealing with true love or trustable and devoted love and not of layman's concept of boyfriend-girlfriend. One person's love can be understood if it is permanent, non-changeable and Love by soul and heart. If it is of physical manner only, it is not a love but it is a lust. Temporary love is just infatuation or Limerence. So, love is the only identity that do not have boundaries or border. It can be inter-religious, inter-caste and between rich and poor. Love identity beyond borders are always criticized by society especially that of conservatives who declared love as non-sense and upheld their 'status' above love identity. They don't recognise the deep feelings and emotions between lovers. They resisted through the use of social norms, like exclusion from family or honour killing.

REFORMS FOR LOVE IDENTITY'S PROTECTION

- Law should prescribe life imprisonment or death sentence for honour killing.
- Person convicted of honour killing should not be provided bail at any cost.
- Legal support should be provided for marriage between completely different identities. Police should not fall in bribe of family members.
- Financial aid and assistance should be given to new couples who belong to different identities at extreme level-for example, between lowest caste and upper most caste, between poorest and richest section, between black people and white people of different race and ethnicity. Integration and unity of Identities through marriage alliances is to be promoted and encouraged.

<u>CONCLUSION</u>

This book has explained the application level of "The Theory of Identities: Social Stratification". A brief summary is given below.

- Don't follow bottom-up approach nor top-down approach. Follow an approach where both are in synthesis but top-down idea should be provided for integrity of identities.
- Women should be empowered but not at the cost of men's right and transgender's life.
- Doctors and engineers should not be considered above other occupations on the basis of merit. They can be considered above illiterate's occupation but not that of identities having same level of education and practicing different profession.
- Different generations should not force their ideas with each other. Instead, advices should be only practised.
- There should not be any partisan in historical identities.
- An identity shall not fall prey to written stereotypes. He shall reject it and complain it to authorities rather than fighting against stereotype.
- 'Love' is the supreme identity; all other identities should be under it.

QUESTION PAPER

These questions are provided as a game to check whether you understood my whole book.

(1) Explain the reforms that has to be taken for protecting love identity.

(2) Prove that there is an unfair legal support to women with some examples.

(3) What are the arguments against historical identity?

(4) The COVID-19 pandemic was made pandemic by the people itself and not by China. Do you agree with the statement? Justify.

(5) Situational identity approach is the best approach. Analyse.

(6) What do you mean by 'positive stereotyping of identities'? Does this 'positive stereotyping' mean that this will yield positive result? Discuss in respect to identity science.

(7) Describe the features of generational identities.

(8) What is the difference between standard and premium identities for an individual? Do you think this is having some relation with economic identity?

(9) Enumerate the advantages and disadvantages of adopting national language model.

(10) The generational identities influence art and culture of a nation. Elaborate.

(11) How does identity defection differ from identity flow and identity tour?

(12) Elucidate the consequence of Identity suicide.

(13) If total generation in place A is 1750 and amount of old generation is 1310, identify the generational density of new generation.

(14) The persons belonging to all-India service is a part of Profession. (Most Easy)

(15) 'Ladies first' saying should be replaced by equal treatment for men and women. Give reason.

(16) List the measures that has to be taken for increasing professionalism in identities.

(17) Internet has played an important role in expanding the scope of identities. Mention at least one Identity that has emerged due to internet.

(18) Adolf Hitler's attitude towards identity was different from those adopted by British. Support the statement with suitable instances.

(19) Examine the push and pull factors for identity improvement and development.

(20) Establish the causes and consequences of stereotyping with identities.

(21) There is a need to strike a balance between gender and religious identity. Comment.

(22) Expound the significance of a role model in the profession before its promotion.

(23) Show the inter-relationship of psychology with identities. Also, review how a generation's thoughts changes with time due to the change in direction of psychology.

EXTRA WORK: Cultural activities can be organised for giving awareness to the people about the use of identities in day-to-day life. It can be done through films or posters.

9 798885 467308